SEASONS OF INSPIRATION

Edited by

Heather Killingray

To John, Christmas 2000.

Small Beginnings!

love

Judith.

First published in Great Britain in 2000 by
POETRY NOW
Remus House,
Coltsfoot Drive,
Woodston,
Peterborough, PE2 9JX
Telephone (01733) 898101
Fax (01733) 313524

HB ISBN 0 75430 945 2
SB ISBN 0 75430 946 0

FOREWORD

Although we are a nation of poets we are accused of not reading poetry, or buying poetry books. After many years of listening to the incessant gripes of poetry publishers, I can only assume that the books they publish, in general, are books that most people do not want to read.

Poetry should not be obscure, introverted, and as cryptic as a crossword puzzle: it is the poet's duty to reach out and embrace the world.

The world owes the poet nothing and we should not be expected to dig and delve into a rambling discourse searching for some inner meaning.

The reason we write poetry (and almost all of us do) is because we want to communicate: an ideal; an idea; or a specific feeling. Poetry is as essential in communication, as a letter; a radio; a telephone, and the main criterion for selecting the poems in this anthology is very simple: they communicate.

CONTENTS

PORTRAIT OF WINTER

So winter is come
  we are alive with the beauty of nature
               revealing her artistry
A mantle of snow in virgin splendour
  softening the contours
            of hill and vale
A sparkle of frost enhancing the landscape
  delighting the eye of all
           who behold the joy
Of evergreens laden with heavy branches
  embroidered with icing
           cottonwool baubles
Nestling as marshmallows - ready for tea
  scarlet of berries glowing, rejoicing
           mistletoe lustrous as pearls
Squatting within their stately hosts
  a new generation sleeps
         under the mantle - waiting
For the palette of nature to paint over
  in pastels shaded
         with the colours of spring.

Eve Salmon

SPRING

Spring steps jauntily in enrobed in hues of green,
The season's dainty, fresh-faced beauty queen,
Trumpeting bright yellow daffodils herald her in,
Winter winds breeze by and the larks start to sing.
The audience of mankind gasp and smile at the sight,
Filling their hearts with joy and delight,
Parading along her glowing smile melting the snow,
Causing the snowdrops and lily of the valley to grow.
Possessing an attitude and vivacity all of her own,
For boldness and resplendence she bears the crown,
A wardrobe of colours, a creative, stunning display,
Tulip red through the crocus purple, an amazing array.
Her model figure, lilting laughter and youthful perfection,
All enhance the wondrously eye-catching collection,
Designer accessories of love, laughter and fun,
The commencement of new life and gentle spring sun.
Her blossom pink cheeks and eyes of hyacinth blue,
Blonde and enticing adorned with diamonds of dew,
Swinging her hips as she leans and then turns,
Fluttering eyelashes playfully behind her fanned ferns.
Leaving the years' catwalk titled as spring,
Gracefully departing as summer drifts in.

Jay Carter

DRAWING CURTAINS

I like to draw the curtains
To greet each brand new morn
To see the changing seasons
That are different every dawn
Spring with its eternal youth
And summer's golden glow
Autumn mists and russet leaves
And winter's pure white snow
I like to draw the curtains
Against the darkening night
As the winter's afternoon
Crowds round my window's light
To hear the clattering rain
Against my windowpane
To sleep, to dream
And in the morn
To greet another brand new dawn

Barbara Anne Smith

INDIAN SUMMER

Here we are, October the first,
white rabbits have been said.
Who would have believed it,
our summer isn't dead.

Three weeks during the summer months
sunshine, cloud free and warm,
then suddenly autumn
and summer was gone.

But very much to our surprise,
the summer has come back
more heat and shining sun daily
with bright, clear blue skies.

They call it an Indian summer
the reason I know not.
Common has been fully searched,
no wigwam could be found.

I McKenzie-Young

SEASONS

I compare thee to a spring morning

Your soul sparkles with the morning dew,
Your being offers purpose in its existence as
pollen does with its seedling.

I compare thee to a summer's day

Your eyes radiate warmth to my soul,
Your hair follows the breath of the breeze,
Your voice comforts my ears like
the calm hum of nature's busy
countryside,
You move with the grace of
brilliant clouds high above.

I compare thee to an autumn evening

Your hands control my ego as it falls to your command
like the crumpled leaves in the wind,
Your lips glow as the sun falls beneath the eternal
horizon.

I compare thee to a winter's night

Your body melts with mine as the cold ebbs away,
Your smile shines through the snow with
immeasurable incandescence.

I D Coxall

SEASONS OF INSPIRATION

Autumn's here, rain and sleet,
Summer is over, gone is the heat,
Leaves are falling like a cloak
Logs on the fire, the smell of smoke,
A conker falls with a gentle thud
Leaving bare the sticky bud.
Apples and pears are gathered in
Stored in the barn in a frost proof bin
The swallows have flown to a foreign clime,
Instinct tells them, this is the time,
Those that stay to brighten the gloom
Search on the lawn where crumbs are strewn.
Snow will soon fall
The children must sledge,
And poke with a broom
Till it falls through the hedge.
The chill of deep winter
The robin's red breast
Of all the four seasons,
It's the one I love best.

Doris M Baker

Autumn In Sutton Park

Earth is soft from August rain, grass stiff and yellow .
In the fall Sutton park is full of life and zest.
Leaves turn orange, brown, whisper to the ground,
Scurry with September gales, then trees begin to rest,

Faint breezes come between the gales to hasten sleep.
Growth lies dormant, ready for chill and snow.
Dogs and owners walk the tracks, joggers pant earnestly.
Through these open spaces voices echo.

Pools lie ruffled by the wind, awaiting visitors from
Northern lands; they feed and shelter on the lake.
The sun has warmth, the skies mottled blue and white.
Swallows gather getting ready for their African trek.

This is the time of fulfilment, fruits abound.
Days they grow shorter, each one more cold.
Walking on crunching leaves, breathing the air,
We gain inner calm, memories of gold.

Jane England

SPRINGTIME

Spring is in the air and the birds are on the wing.
Love twitters thro the trees
And the blackbirds begin to sing.
Pretty blue forget-me-nots and golden daffodils
Make a lovely scene.
The lambs are prancing in the fields
So, come on, let us all shout spring, spring, spring.
Out comes my hat, now fancy that,
Ribbons and lace, to cheer up my face.
I am certain that this rhyme
Will make you want to sing, sing, sing.

E Colyer

DAFFODILS

Through the narrow glen and mead
Carpeted in gold
Yielding sun and warmth to all
Reveals to us in magnitude
Our hidden treasures of the earth.
Gentle breezes through the lea
Where streamlets run the course of time
Heralds the trumpets of the spring
The daffodils.

Anne Christabel Davey-Young

VIEW FROM A WINDOW

Gossamer threads, strands of silver delight
Weaved by invisible hands through the night
Spiders' webs draped over branches held high
Like filigree lace under colour-washed sky
Gleaming like moonstones reflecting the light.

Nuthatches, robins and sparrows take flight
Deterred by a magpie declaring his might
And filling the air with his harsh, strident cry,
Shattering the world made of gossamer.

Sunlight breaks through, jewelled dewdrops shine bright
Then splash onto grass crisply frosted and white.
Muddled thoughts turn to wishes, they soar and then fly
On the breeze, in the slipstream, then fall, gently sigh.
They dance round my dreams, fears recede, all seems right
Unshed tears cloud my eyes like gossamer.

Sheila Hussey

SEPTEMBER SUBTLETY

A mellow amber opulence endowed
successor to the summer scene,
timorous autumn, gifted with a cloud,
abundance of rich tint,
its saving grace,
with power to imprint,
take pride of place,
indelible gold glint,
earth to embrace,
paint the threatening dark
with luminous red spark,
September's gratifying glow
with winter warily in tow.

It might be any time of day or night,
December, June or early May,
when my thinking mesmeric, takes flight,
brings autumn to the fore,
one special hour
I conjure up with awe,
precious bower
in garden I adore,
radiant shower
displaying crimson cloak
of blossom; no one spoke
and no one sang but ardent thrush
embellishing that autumn hush.

Ruth Daviat

ALL IS NOT LOST

Oh! Just look, at our Yorkshire weather, so cold, so damp with a
Touch of frost,
The ground is slippy with icy patches, the damp's set in, but
All is not lost,
It won't be long before spring is upon us, and the lambs all jumping
In the air,
Then comes along summer, that makes us feel younger, so carefree,
Happy without a care,
Then autumn comes and before you know it, you're reaching out again
For woollies and thick socks.
It seems a blink of an eye, then winter's back on us, another year
Older, but all is not lost,
I would not leave Yorkshire, whatever the weather, with its cold,
Damp and that touch of frost,
I'm alive! And that's all that matters, I can't grumble, and health,
Not too bad, for this Yorkshire lass,
So whatever the weather, with seasons in regions, Yorkshire's
Lucky, just to have that wintry frost,
And whenever I'm down, tired and weary, I remember the
Seasons, then say,
'Oh, well, all is not lost!'

Mary Shaw-Taylor

SEASONS OF INSPIRATION

The mystic feel of the Highlands
Mah bonny wee heather
set in the Glen
Energy flowing from the ground
and in the air,
I could walk the Highlands
without care.
Taking in deep lungfulls of air
gazing at the horizon
Is it to be fair?
Clouds rolling by
as I silently stare.
Smiling happily as I walk
grouse flying overhead
nature all around.
A slight mist rising from the bog
the beauty of life.
It came from God.

Julian Thorpe

THE WAITING LAND

Behold the solemn winter moon,
Which shines upon a captive land,
Revealing sedge adorned with frost,
Proud glittering spikes in tidy ranks.
While daggers of ice hang poised
Where last year's lustrous mayflies loved and lost.

Sweet copper globe proclaims the dawn,
A battle fought and bravely won,
To burn through steely morning mist:
Igniting naked silver trees,
Releasing water held in thrall.
A worthy ally to enlist.

At noon a pallid silver disc,
Peers shyly through the freezing fog.
Now, atmospheric swords are crossed,
And dove-grey clouds release their load,
To drift wildly over dormant earth,
Concealing last night's deadly frost.

Still, evening brings a precious gift,
A setting sun of burnished gold,
A ray of hope, a vital force,
Now bronze upon the snow capped hills,
A promise that burns set hard like stone,
Will soon resume their downward course.

And when the silent moon returns,
To view this strangely tranquil scene,
Small creatures watch with baited breath,
For buds to stir and streams to flow.
As spring unlocks the waiting land,
To end this graceful transient death.

Sandra Hopwood

SUMMER

Have you seen the sunlight, shining through the branches on a lovely summer's day?
Have you see the blue of the cloudless sky that seems to never want to go away?
Have you watched the birds, riding on the thermals, just cruising round and round?
Have you watched the swans on the river, drifting without a sound?
Have you smelt the roses in bloom with colours of every hue?
And have you smelt the honeysuckle, as its perfume comes wafting through?
Have you watched the bumble bees, getting nectar from the flowers?
Have you felt the peace that hovers in the summer's evening hours?
Have you seen the range of flowers in the gardens that you pass by?
Have you ever watched the sunset in a balmy summer evening sky?
And have you heard excited children playing in the sea and sand?
Have you watched the rabbits playing in the fields, in
England's green land?
Have you ever made rainbows from the water of the hose pipe spray?
And have you tried to eat a chocolate ice cream, before it melts away?
That's summer!

June Bootle

Spring Time

Winter had been long and hard;
Cruel wind and biting frost:
Forced to stay within my room,
Sorrow filled my heart and gloom
That nature's joys seemed lost.

But going out one sunny day,
My heart began to sing:
I saw in that enchanted hour,
Nature's bright creative power;
The mysteries of spring.

Alexander K Sampson

CRICKET - OR NOT!

Spring's flown away and with good reason
It's the start of cricket's season.
Noble game of bat and ball,
As English as the cuckoo's call,
Traditional fight of willow and leather,
Fair play's the thing - given the weather!
In theory, skies are always blue.
In practice, grey's the normal hue.
Clouds roll in and brollies bloom
To point upturned at deepening gloom.
The rain begins, drops by the million
Chase players into the pavilion
Covers go on - it's looking grim
And naturally, the light is dim.
Spectators, gone into their huddles,
Contemplate enlarging puddles.
Then loudspeakers, crackling, say
'Play is abandoned for the day.'
All trudge off home, tired, cold and wet
But one thing makes them happy, yet.
Though hands are numb and feet are numb-er
They can be sure it's English summer!

R P Brown

MIRACLE OF SPRING

Spring is a time, of all things new
Crisp fresh mornings, grass covered in dew
Lambs are born, they frolic around
Daffodils, bluebells, shoot up from the ground
Birds call their mates, with a twittering tune
Owls call their mates by the light of the moon
It's the start of a new life, for the birds and bees
Little green shoots on bushes and trees
Frogspawn and tadpoles in ponds and lake
Hibernating hedgehogs finally wake
Howls and whistles, mating calls abound
The mating calls of she-cat to hound
They come from afar, north, south, east or west
Rummaging, scurrying with bedding for a nest
From puppies, kittens, lambs, calves, birds unfurled
The life of spring is brought to this world
A badger in his set to a bird in his tree
This miracle of spring, is for all to see.

Carl Fricker

SEASONS AT THE COTTAGE

I would love a cottage in *Springtime*
When all nature is born anew
And little lambs go frolicking
In fields of verdant hue
And crocuses and daffodils
In bright array adorn the hills.

I would love a cottage in *Summer*
With roses by the door
With a quaint old bench to sit upon
To watch the skylark soar
And listen to the honey bees
A-humming round the flowers and trees.

I would love a cottage in *Autumn*
When the fields are ripe with corn
And the farmer gathers his harvest in
And gives thanks - on Sunday morn
In the little church - by the old oak tree
Now decked in its glorious majesty.

I would love a cottage in *Winter*
When the trees are stark and bare
And an icy wind brings snowflakes
Twirling and swirling everywhere
And a robin sings on the garden gate
And a fire burns cheerily in the grate.

Yes, I'd love a cottage in Springtime
In Summer, Winter or Fall
But I'd really love it best of all
When you would come and call
And chat with me a little while
And share the sunshine of your smile.

Jean Millar

A TRIFLE COLD

The wild winter now draws forth its bow, and providence describes
The thrifty squirrel its larder nests, and tests all lesser tribes.
Ah thou spectral skies, wert telling lies, storm fettered winds o'ercast,
Commanding in wrath, with fearful might, dark light that last and last.

Ah winds basely cleft, carelessly left, and tormented and tost,
Art blowing away the shifting sun, undone, and sorely lost.
Art thou, straining trees, complaining seas, confounded now, unblest,
Surreptitiously in mournful wake, doth quake, with angry zest.

Oh those summer days, when sunshine plays on everything around,
E'er rippling abroad its arrowed heat, to beat on vibrant ground.
Oh these languid hours, of hazy showers, fain mirroring across,
And sprinkling the skies its tinsle beams, rich dreams and heav'ly dross.

Oh those lazy clinks of cool iced drinks, and strawberry made fare,
Wast sweetest perfume in all the world, unfurled, and wafted there.
Oh great canopy above of me, so petulant, so high,
Canst pour forthwith that liquid gold, and mould a warmer I.

Derek Haskett-Jones

SUPERB ADVENTURE

I never considered my life to be
A superb adventure, that is until
A day last month, a day in May.
The red and white hawthorns were heavy
And redolent with blossom; the lime
Leaves were tenderly bright green
And the Queen Anne's lace frothy and
So decorative; stocks, in the garden,
Breathed delightful perfume - and these
Joys were just in Suffolk! How could
I not believe in eternal life among
Such bounty? How could my love of
Flower and tree, lane and meadow
Not be carried into a loving heaven!

Elizabeth Brown

SEASONAL LIFE AND DEATH

Each year begins in sterile mood
the land seems barren grey,
yet winter feeds emerging shoots
that filter through decay.

The early blooms of springtime
melt the starkness of the earth,
a tangled pyre their backcloth,
a shower of gems their birth.

The annual surge of sap and leaf
is born of milder breath,
whose conditions yield abundance,
its decline forewarning death.

And changing hues of autumn leaves
display a mellowed sight,
their life a darkened canopy,
their death a golden light.

Susan Turner

UNIVERSAL PLIGHT

Stars set the night like a space
Without universal horizons

Until waves of darkness
On the dawning shores of light

Carry planet earth from oblivion
To do business with the sun

And the seasons.

Marylène Walker

Summer And Autumn

The summer brings the sun and warmth.
Birds lay eggs and wait for birth.
Swallows glide, swoon and fly,
Like aeroplanes in combat for the skies.
Catching insects that pass them by.

Farmers cut and bale the hay.
Fodder for the livestock,
Come winter's harshest day.
Children getting off from school,
For their annual summer hols.
Two whole months to run around and play.
Excursions to the seaside,
Ice cream, sweets and candy floss,
And not forgetting donkey rides.

Autumn brings the winds that,
Strip the trees of leaves,
And also brings the cool and gentle breeze.
The apples, plums and pears,
Are ready to be picked.
Hallowe'en is here again.
The children play their tricks.
The bonfires glow so bright,
Against the dark, black sky.
'A penny for the guy'
You can hear the kiddies cry.
The squirrels gather nuts,
For winter hibernation.
It has always been the custom,
One of nature's old traditions.

Stephen Martin

AUTUMN

A season full of waiting,
as winter takes its grasp,
and yet a sense of longing
for other times, now past.

Summer's leaves begin to fall
into the wooded glade.
A rich and dappled river
beneath its dying shade.

Winter's icy fingers reach
into its darkening day.
Etching frosted pictures,
where summer's flowers lay.

The time of nature's change,
rich with amber and gold.
A definite sense of age,
but not altogether old.

Rebecca Coombs

SEASONS

Wake up your day
The nights are long
The days are grey
The winter is here
The sun is at bay.
The spring will arrive
With a little warm glow
But before it comes
We will likely have snow.
Snow is like a blanket
Covering the ground
Warming dormant seeds all around.
The forces of nature
Will rear their heads
To greet another season
With many flower beds.
The sap will rise
To the tallest tree
The cycle continues
For you and me.
The world will go on
For ever and ever
As long as people
Don't get too clever.
The die was cast long ago
Wake up your day
Get up and go!

James Rodger

SUMMER IN THE CITY

Hey! Fever Time

Summer in the city
Ain't always very pretty
Sneezing
Wheezing
Hoards of flies
Itchy eyes
Prickly heat
Smelly feet
Light nights
Gnat bites
Bare chest
Skimpy vest
Garbage stink
Too much drink
Hot house trains
Blocked up drains
Skin peeling
Restless feeling.

Joan Vicente

FROST FILIGREE

Winter sun beams on the stillness
of the garden, starched with frost,
the sloping steps, ice trap for the unwary,
shimmer with rainbow colours in the light;
the night has scattered profusion
of diamonds as from a broken necklace
on the lawn, left them as gift
for morning to discover and collect.

A thrush sings out her golden liquid notes
in pure clear air that catches her melodies
and sets them dancing around the trees,
through filigree of grass and fern and flower;
the castor oil plant, sentry at the gate,
stands straight, stiff and correct as the doorman at The Ritz -
and equally attentive when tits come foraging and find
her last remaining seeds held high for hungry beaks.

Now on the frozen road the sand the lorries laid
while neighbours slept, leaps up to meet the tyres
of slowly driving cars workward bound
through rushing city streets,
leaving reluctantly behind the magic wonderland
of frosted shapes and silent sounds
of the winter garden
shining in the January sun.

Oonagh Twomey

THE SUMMER IS HERE

The summer is here, flowers starting to grow
The birds starting to go with the flow
Then slide and glide down to the ground
Where food can be seen as well as found.

The sun is shining, the rain has gone
Now all the animals feel that they belong
With the sun shining it's never really night
Where in winter it is hardly ever daylight.

Families and couples are walking out and about
Children playing on the beach starting to shout
Building sandcastles along with sand pies too
Paddling in the sea that is very blue.

Holiday time has arrived again, people out late
Nice weather means ice-cream on a plate
Hot days is the time to laze and daze
Then seagulls come to look and gaze.

Coleen Bradshaw

SEASONS OF INSPIRATION

Oh to be in England,
Now that spring is here
Oh to see the snowdrops
And daffodils appear.

To see the great awakening
Of flowers and trees around
And all the signs of life appear
From gardens all around.

There's nothing quite like daffodils
To welcome in the spring
These cheerful little nodding heads
Do so much pleasure bring.

They start the lovely programme
Of flowers all through the year
Which bring us so much pleasure
And give us so much cheer.

The wonder of the seasons
Fill us with delight
The lovely sun in summer
The snow in winter bright.

The dawning of a summer morn
The setting of the sun
The awesome sound of thunder
Which startles everyone.

And so the seasons come and go
And give us so much pleasure
And make so many happy years
For all of us to treasure.

A Kendall

SPRING TIME

Spring is in the air so clean and refreshing
With that sparkling feeling of a new awakening
The joy and warmth of being born again
Game to tackle anything in sunshine or rain
As Mother Nature opens her doors
To the birds and wildlife as she quietly lures
Them out of hibernation
Into the countryside now, alive in God's creation
When the trees and shrubs burst their buds once again born
After the dark days and into a new dawn
With the winter months now out of sight
Welcoming another season of spring time so bright
On the 21st of March with breezes quite shrill
Sweeping over a carpet of primroses and daffodils
Into April with showers of rain
Gently spraying those seeds sown to be born again
From springtime until the harvest hive
Of crops and plants that will hopefully survive,
Together with the baby lambs so woolly and warm
A welcome sign of spring time so happy to be born
Whilst scampering around the meadow so bold
Where the mayflowers bloom alongside the marsh marigold
A picturesque scene of spring time at last
As Mother Nature recycles God's big field so vast.

Nancy Owen

SHADES OF AUTUMN

Beautiful Autumn
Berries aplenty
Red ones and yellow
In spotlighted sun.

Burnished gold bushes
And canopied trees
Soon they'll be laid bare
Wind rustling their leaves.

Low lie the sun's rays
Long lie the shadows
Shades of the Autumn
Red, russet and gold.

Helen Sharpe

Autumn

Nuanced amber entices to learn,
Where deciduous trees beleave in turn,
That nature is prepared to burn,
Through auroral hope and occident concern,
In a perpetual season of evenings yearn.

Anthony John Ward

SAFE FROM THE STORM

Hurry! Hurry!
Fly and scurry
Like a demon in the night,
Again! Again!
Beat your rain
Up against the windowpane,
Fill my heart with willing fright.

Thunder, thunder,
Tear asunder,
All the world outside the room,
Lightening, lightening
Children frightening,
Fill the world with fear of doom.

Cosy, cosy
Warm and rosy,
All my fears have taken flight,
I'm not weeping,
For I'm sleeping,
In my parent's bed tonight.

Tony Coyle

EASTER IN THE FOREST

We walk along the woodland track, the trees now clothed in green
The primrose and the bluebell add such colour to the scene
The kids play in the puddles as the cyclists ride on by
Eventually the sun breaks through the dark clouds in the sky
At last the rainstorm eases off, though the wind cuts like a knife
The bird songs echo through the trees as the forest comes to life
We get back to the car park and eat our picnic there
The birds all hop around the car, our food they want to share
The nuthatch and the robin, the chaffinch and the tits
All squabble over crumbs we throw and pick up all the bits
A buzzard circles overhead, a squirrel climbs a tree
The children run around the grass as happy as can be
We take them to the playground and let them just run free
Whilst us adults sit and chatter and drink our flasks of tea
You can't predict the weather, nor what the day will bring
But there's nothing like a good long walk in a forest in the spring.

Steve Harris

SUMMER IN MY GARDEN

I've dug some potatoes for dinner, the weeds in the
                                   veg patch look thinner,
Watered the beans and picked some too. My nails are a sight
They'd give you a fright, I can't garden with gloves on, can you?
Flowers are a picture, the lawn full of sun. For now I think
                                   my gardening's done
It's getting hot, no breath of air. Everything's quiet, nobody there
I think for now I'll have a rest. Oh! I've just spotted a garden pest
A snail, I'll have to get rid of him. Won't kill him, just put
                                   him in the compost bin
He can live there a while amongst a great pile of rubbish he'd
                                   likely call dinner
He'll survive, may even thrive. For sure he won't get any thinner
Now I'll chop down some elder and briar. A wild hedge
                                   is surely better than wire
Some tomatoes are ready, cucumbers as well. The home
                                   grown taste you can tell
Must check the blackberries while I'm here. Crumble time is very near
Just very gently shake a branch. Surprise, surprise, quite by chance
Big juicy ones fall into your hand. These ones I'll eat.
                                   Oh! They're grand
Time flies when you're enjoying yourself. Think about dinner,
                                   what's on the shelf
No need, the garden will provide. I'll take a basketful inside
Potato, bean, cucumber, tomato and snail salad with
                                   blackberry crumble for afters.

Mary Alison

SEASONS

Winter is here again, the seasons of
Coldness, dull and dark.

Spring is here, new life, flowers,
Animals and trees.

Summer is hot, hot, hot, hot.
The days get longer and warmer.

Autumn is here again.
Season of conkers and falling leaves.

George Smith (9)

SUMMERTIME

Summertime a sheet
of heat distorted vision.
Red warmth under the eyelids.
Lazy moments of shimmering time.

A bee drones by
sucks the yellow out of summer.
Echoes the dreamy haze
which belongs to remembrances
of these golden days.

Ruth Goode

THE PRICE OF PEACE

The sun, yes the sun
So warm it's golden rays
Shines on the wark that God has done
Where he still often strays.

The dawn, yes the dawn
It's not so welcome now
There's heartaches wake with every morn
And lines of weary on our brow.

The war, yes the war
A battle, but not with sword
Like the Christians, we go onward
To die for Britain, for British we are.

The peace, yes the peace
We'll win it in the end
We have much faith in the men we send
To fight for us for peace.

Let us all be well content
With the beauties of the spring
The dawn, the sun, that God has sent
And the birds in the trees that sing.

When we start to moan and groan
For something that is scarce
Just stop to think, when you're alone
Of brave men who do not curse
Because the fighting does not cease
But bravely die, so we have peace.

Grace Wallace

SUN CITY

Ladybird clockwork giggles,
Swallows skate the sky,
Windows yawn, sills greet elbows,
Chimney's holiday
Tarmac wobbly fairground mirrors,
Hot tin roofs perspire,
Docked doctored cuts and stings,
Daisy chain attire,
Sticky fingers, sunlicked faces,
Water fighting yells,
Beaten rugs from fireplaces,
Ice cream jingle bells,
Dragging drowsy dogs for walkies,
Baby's pushchair treat,
'Don't go far . . . stay on the pavement,'
Mothers' rest their feet.
Washing basket, dollies table,
Dark secrets blanket den,
Teatime buttered sandwiches,
Bellies full again.
Washing's dry, table's turning,
Mother's scrutiny,
Bathtub running, footsteps coming,
Children's mutiny,
Stretching shadows, windows shutting,
Pink-ribboned, turquoise sky,
Docile deckchair, juice-spent beaker,
Blackbird's lullaby.

Liz Burns

COUNTRY SUMMER

Summer - just sitting in the garden
Under the old apple tree,
My cup of tea quite near me,
My book ready on my knee -
Each page waiting to be read at leisure
Reading, not weeding is my pleasure.

Looking at the flowers - waving in the breeze,
Watch the bees humming
Birds twittering in the trees
Savouring precious moments, having a little doze,
Until the spell is shattered
With the manure smell - up my nose!

Vera Homer

SUMMER'S HERE

'Where've you been I missed you?' little Danny said one day
as he shouted to the sunshine who'd returned from far away.
'It's been so cold without you, it's been wind and rain and sleet,
I had to wear a hat and gloves, and big boots on my feet.'

But sunshine didn't answer
he just shone with all his might.

'Mum will make fresh lemonade, to take down to the park,
'I might stay up all night long because it wouldn't get dark.
Dad will take me fishing, I'll climb trees and have some fun
All the people smiling now that summer's just begun.'

But sunshine didn't answer
He just faded in his glow.

'Grandad will weed the garden, then water all the flowers
And I'll play with the hose pipe outside I'll stay for hours.
We'll all go to the seaside, wet sand between our toes,
Then laugh at grandma with ice cream on her nose.'

But sunshine didn't answer
He just hid behind a cloud.

'Now Danny,' said his mother, 'Who you shouting to out there?'
'The people in that bus stop, they have begun to stare,'
'You can't shout at the sunshine you'll frighten him away,'
'This is Lancashire we live in, summer only lasts a day . . .'

Lynn Noblett

DO YOU KNOW YOUR MESSENGER?

The question I ask to which no answer lies,
Is what else will we see with our eyes?
Seeing is believing and the belief must be true,
You've seen your world through and through.

So take a moment so you can inspire,
Your body, mind and soul to Gaia.
Your messenger knows you, but do you know him?
You will as soon as your soul light turns dim.

At that precise instance your life will be unearthed,
The path will be shown through which many have surfed.
Such sights to show, such beauty to touch,
For most and many it's all too much!

Your messenger will guide your virgin eyes,
Through the pleasant place where doubt dies.
Free your mind, it's the souls right to breath,
Freedom is what you will receive.

Daniel Compton

THOUGHTS OF SUMMER

I think of summertime
With loving thoughts
The smell of roses and
Forget me nots.

Lazy days on the river
As the sun beats down
Swans swim past with
Signets all around.

Smells of cherry blossom
Brings love to mind
Scents captivating me in
Many different kinds.

The air is alive with
Birdsong butterfly and bee
Lazy hazy summer days
Just for you and me.

Lovers holding hands stroll
Along the shore
As the waves wash in and
Out once more.

Memories forever to behold
For me
Warm loving thoughts just
By the sea.

Marilyn Davidson

SPRING

The air is filled with the scents of spring
As the earth from its troubled sleep,
Push the tender green leaves to a sky above
Where awaiting sun now peeps.
For this awakening is a miracle
That only God can make,
So that everyone in this universe with eager hands can take -
A share of these joys to please our eyes
And fill our hearts with love
Makes everything in life worthwhile
Has come from him above.
Like the tinkle of the laughter
From a child who is running free
After the long cold days of winter
These belong to you and me.
And to look on a tiny new born life
From the warmth of its mother's womb
Are lent to us all, from the cycle of life
Each year, but goes so soon.
So enjoy this spring in its newest gown
And the earth in its sweet parade,
Hold out your hands and take your fill
Before this miracle fades.

Ivy Gallimore

AWAKENING

Not long now, not long before the sun shines again,
The crimson beams may still be concealed,
But the potential looming glory is bursting to explode,
This Godly beauty will soon be revealed.

Push me in the right direction,
Take me now to new dimensions,
Let us all release our tensions,
Let me swim in crystal streams,
We will live out all our dreams.

It's nearly there, not long before the clouds have died away,
The people are still subdued, held tight in God's clenched fist,
But the awakening will encompass us all soon
And our restraints will all be dispersed into the mist.

Show me youthful freedom in parkland pleasures,
Guide me to shining, urban treasures,
Take me to see marvellous magic tides,
River rafts flowing gracefully, a surfer glides,
Minds mingling as winter's gloom hides.

Look up everyone, look around, hear the sounds,
Hear the calming, soothing trill
Ease from rows of contented birch,
Feel the soft, angelic breeze, sweep kindly onto your face,
See the evergreen maze that intrigues,
Explore and discover that forgotten place,
This time has come, this summer time grace.

It's all come now, I'm a statue, rooted beneath
                            these summer time rays,
Let's hope this awesome wonder stays,
All life and activity is showing,
When the summer subsides, falters and dies,
Let's hope the glittering streams are still flowing.

Simon Cardy

DIFFERENT SEASON

Well the end of March is nearly here
Gone are the dark nights until later this year,
When it's cold and dark nothing seems to get done
We feel so much better when we see the sun.
I know we will get some days when it pours with rain
But I am looking forward to doing the garden again.
The lawns are now ready to start to mow,
I now feel ready at having a go.
I cannot believe there are butterflies about
And all the shrubs and trees are all sprouting out.
The crocuses have gone until next time around.
There's always different things growing out the ground
All the birds sit chirping high up in the trees,
The buds have started opening to show their new green leaves,
It's a lovely time of year now that winter's really gone
And feel the temperature rising as the time goes on.

Colin H Cross

SUMMER HEAT

S   un rays bring happy hours
U   nfolding petals from sleepy flowers
M ellowing in the light of the warmth heat
M emories sharing to all we meet
E   njoying the illuminated light
R   est assured their days are right.

David Brewer

ONE TURN ON THE CLOCK

Chills, winds, aches and pains
Never-ending hails and rains.
But now, see the globe has spun
Heralding a new season's return
Not now a short day, a long night
Instead, a new way, an evening bright.

Walks, sports, all kinds of fun.
Children at play under the sun.
Plans, too, for taking a break
To a small chalet down by a lake.
Where a wisp of smoke trails from a stack
Time has stood still here, neither forward nor back.

Trees, hedges, flowers in bloom
A shaft of light into the room
Out in the fields the beasts do graze.
Offspring close by, dancing in the haze
The portrait complete, a sight to behold
Summer re-born, bringing joy ten-fold.

Alick MacDonald

HOT DAYS

Spring has sprung,
Summer's here,
It's begun,
Hot days.
Barbecue craze.
Cool, refreshing drink
Summer's brilliant,
I think
Lots to do
Must have fun
Sand and sea
Paddling for me,
Something nice for tea
Strawberries and cream
A summer dream
It's a wonderful time of year
And everyone's glad, it's finally here,
I wish summer, would last forever,
Me, I'm going to really enjoy
Myself whatever.

Caroline Janney

SUMMER THOUGHTS

The mixed sweet smelling aroma that
Travels with the breeze.
From newly cut grass and flowers
The blossom on the trees.

The warm lingering sensation as the
Sun caresses your face,
Like a greeting with a loved one
When you kiss and then embrace.

The salty spray from the ocean
As the waves spill into shore,
The soft fine sand beneath my
Feet, a feeling that I adore.

The twitter of birds chatting
Bustling around and building nests,
The butterflies gracefully gliding
Above colourful flowerbeds.

The coolness of the night air says
She will not be here for long, so
Take advantage of the summer and
Keep your thoughts with you year long.

Linda Gooden

SUMMERTIME

S   ummertime awakes at last, as from
U   nder her new and colourful cape,
M   ultitudes of changes begin to take shape.
M   onths of darkness are a thing of the past, as
E   arth unveils its new summer look, a
R   iot of colour explodes as buds burst free,
T   ulips and daffodils waving their heads for all to see,
I   n the meadows, water plays in the clean, clear brook.
M   emories of dark dismal days are now long gone as
E   very new day is filled with glorious bird song.

S Revell

THE THOUGHTS OF SUMMER

The crisp warm smell around us,
The long grass where we run,
The picnics by the water,
The lovely summer sun.

The streets are filled with people,
The flowers are in bloom,
The gardens are all beautiful,
The lawns need cutting soon.

The smiles on all our faces,
The glow we feel inside,
The days that last forever,
The joy I cannot hide.

The barbecues and funny games,
The splashing in the pool,
The parties that can last all day,
The men that act like fools.

The day has nearly ended,
The sun has gone away,
The children now have gone to bed,
The end of a perfect day.

Lynne Harrison

VACATION VOYAGE

Is sailing on the ocean wave
Reserved for sea-dogs, strong and brave?
No, callow tourists too, may sail
On azure seas, no storm or gale
To islands with their sandy coves
And anchor in the cool, calm bays,
Then snorkel in the turquoise deep
Returning to the decks to sleep;
Whilst in the galley fruit is pared
And cheese and wine and bread are shared
Then, anchor weighed and engine primed,
The vessel starts the voyage back
To mainland harbour -sultry, hot,
And moored by dinghy, boat or yacht,
Happily tired, the sailors new
Offer their thanks to the crew,
And stagger from the tranquil sea,
They slip their moorings easily
To find an English cup of tea!

Heather A Hayne

THOUGHTS OF SUMMER

Awake to a new summer's dawn, with all the promise
Of youth and beauty.
These first days of summer, being new and fresh and unspoilt by the
Still heat of mid summer nights, and far away from the long,
Dark sleep of winter time.

J B Burton

A Family Day Out By The Sea

Suntan lotion, lolly sticks
Children laughing having fun
Funny hats with kiss me quick
Parents soaking up the sun
Granpa paddling in the sea
Trousers rolled up to his knees
A man says, 'Like your photo taken dear?'
But gran pretends not to hear
Auntie sulked quite a bit
Because her bikini did not fit
Uncle, children minus socks
Played amongst the pools and rocks
Mother said, 'It's nearly three
All gather round for tea.'
Ham sandwiches, pickle, cheese
Lemonade made baby sneeze
Hard boiled eggs and salad cream
Followed by a chocolate dream
Danny had a runny nose
Cried with sand between his toes
Baby looking hot and red
Had pushed his bonnet off his head
Packed and dressed, they caught a train
Promising the children they'd come again.

F H G Fuller

SUMMER

Where the evening draws out the light
The earth is green and coloured bright
The sun warms the darkest hole
To heat and comfort every soul
The fields are alive with aroma and song
As children happy, dance and play along
The martin skips through the golden hay
While for others, shade is sought to cool the day
As bumble bee's and butterflies keenly display
While gathering the pollen in further fields to lay
But in a haste this season is soon to end
For autumn with its changes sends.

Richard McPartlan

MAY AND JUNE

Ah! May and June, May and June,
When the hedges are thick
With buds and bees
And the bright sharp shine
Of the fresh green leaves.
When we might dance
Through the sunny glades
Or steal an hour
From an endless year
To share beneath
The dappled shade.
When nothing is owed
And nothing is sad,
When the flowers unfold
With promises set,
When the evenings long
May longer be
For the glow to hold
To eternity,
In May and June.

If nothing was owed
And nothing was sad,
Why have those days
So swiftly fled?

Tom Thurston

THOUGHTS OF SUMMER

When my thoughts turn to summer
I become quite dreamy, and smile
I can feel the sun on my face
And I stop what I'm doing for a while.

I can smell the ribs on the barbecue
And taste the juicy steak
The chilled white wine is delicious
I really don't want to wake.

Friends are chatting together
I'm feeling relaxed and carefree
There is no feeling quite like it
When the world just stops for me.

The air is alive with laughter
Everyone is feeling high
These balmy days of summer
Not a cloud in the deep blue sky.

Time to end the dream
Back to reality for me
I'm actually shaking with cold
Well it's only February.

Karen Leigh Brown

SIX WEEKS

End of the term,
Quiet in schools,
Empty clean classrooms,
There are no rules -
For six weeks.

No dull, grey uniform,
Black, regulation shorts,
No history lessons,
Or compulsory sports -
For six weeks.

Freedom from marking
Staying in bed,
Potter in the garden,
No thoughts in one's head -
For six weeks.

Beaches and candyfloss,
Sun, sand and sea,
No pupils to care for,
I'll just think of me -
For six weeks.

Wendy Beckett

SUMMER ARRIVING

Summer time is here once more
Our days get long and bright
We thank God for the morning
And pray to him each night

The sun shines across the meadow
And lambs have turned to sheep
The nights are getting hotter
We find it hard to sleep

We love the many flowers
Grown well into full bloom
It makes the land so pretty
And takes away the gloom

We feel we are ready for summer
The sun it perks us up
We get out the cakes and biscuits
And pour the tea in our cup

Oh for the summer to stay
But we know that winter will come
We pack away our garden tools
And know our gardening's done.

C Swain

MOONSHINE

Past meadow and pasture, past beasts of the fields
'neath haven of heaven where bittern wheels
through shimmering tracery of silvery stream
glides the 'Gladadriel', the moonshine dream.

Where amber meets crystal with relaxing power
Where lasher and lock her progress devour
and hostelry jetty safe refuge provides
or your 'ail gartref'; at her anchor rides.

Moth and butterfly and dragonfly too
buzz by the banks in sky of bright blue.

Coot and duck and moorhen and swan
amend their journey as moonshine drifts on,
then rush and reed and teasel topped stem
nod in approval as her wake caresses them.

Rippling gently onward with adagio speed
the quiet corners of your conscious to feed
Through the abdomen of nature, gliding free.
Oh! Perfect moonshine your ambrosia she.

Dave Double

SUNSHINE WHERE ARE YOU?

Hold me in your skies of flamboyant sunshine
As the loneliness blinds me,
With cold teardrops crushed
Into white powdery rain.

So burn the thunder that's
Lighting my heart
- With so much pain.
And thaw the remains of
The sludge upon my boots.

So let me cruise in your galaxies
Of comets, and ride upon
The spheres as they orbit,
Around the cooling, warming sun
- My once alone heart calls . . .

For this explosion, I've been witnessed
To too much exposure,
Of sweet, sugar lumps that sparkle shiny stars.
And the night-time wolf sings
me a song, from the mystery lover's eye.

Moon you seem curiously friendly, as your shadow
Hides and curtains my knight,
- That's armour naturally shines.
Won't you feel pity, and love thy as yours?
Why won't my sunshine
Reply to my wiltering calls?

Ann Worrell

JUST A THOUGHT

Clear blue skies
Stretch as far as the eye can see
Warm sun on your face
With the odd gentle breeze:
summer thoughts enter my head
As I lie relaxing on my bed:
Waking on a sunlit morn
Open windows welcome the dawn
Sounds of birdsong on the lawn.
Ideal summer thoughts:

Strolling thro' fields of poppies and wheat
Take in the fresh air
With the grass for a seat.
Hearing the ripple of the water's edge
Running back and forth on the beach.
Sand and shingle beneath the toes
In summer the stress goes.
Happiness - laughter
The humming of the bee
Like nature to all summer is free.

Julie Powell

VILLAGE DAYS
(1914-1918)

Three sunny summers - this I know is true,
History books record it - we would play
We six to ten year olds, the long day through,
The war in Europe was a world away.

No longer safe, our well-known North Sea coast,
And so we went, as autumn term drew near,
On holiday, some forty miles at most;
The small small cottage welcomed us each year.

The village shop held treasures; you could buy
For one old penny, sweets or balls, or toys
Of celluloid, dog, cat, cow, swan, chose I,
Elephant, lion, tiger were for boys!

Hanging Stone Rocks we'd visit, up the hills;
A penny or two was all the entrance fee.
We'd climb, play hide and seek or roam at will
On sheep-cropped turf with bracken tall as me.

How sweet its scents, how clear the summer sky,
How gaily sang the skylarks overhead!
How wide and safe it seemed! And there nearby
The small wild raspberries were turning red.

And other haunts we had: steep Beacon Hill -
(A narrow belt of trees beside its lane,
Though open, scared me - had some ancient ill
There chanced? I never asked, so fears remain) -

The road where tiny frogs leapt up a tree -
The wild flowers, campion, knapweed, margarite -
My mother's gingerbread for picnic tea -
And blessing all, the gentle summer heat.
Does happy childhood cast a rosy glow?
Why then, how lucky I to have it so!

Kathleen M Hatton

How Does Your Garden Grow?

Canterbury bells delicately shaped as cups and saucers,
Dianthus pinks, dressed in frills like pretty daughters,
Delphiniums, lupins, shooting heavenward as pointed spires;
We kneel to candytufts their colour to admire.

Full bosomed peonies, the sweetly coloured rose
Attract the senses to point the nose.
Weeping fuchsia spills blood red colour on path,
Daffodils and tulips lie in trenches under grass.

Heavy scented honeysuckle's pink tipped fingers twine around,
Green leafed clematis, purple golden crowned, regally gowned,
Flag iris, stiff geranium heads ramrod as soldiers;
Whilst velvet faced pansies gaze on as beholders.

Chirping bird, droning bee cooled by breeze,
Dappled shade across the grass, whispering trees,
Sounds of water rippling from a stream,
Makes an English garden a summer's dream.

K D Netherton

APRIL WISHES

In the summer I hope the sun
will split the trees.
I hope there will be
stacks of bumble bees,
and grass going
brown from heat
and red hot paving
slabs for bare feet.
Thunderstorms with
half crown rain drops.
Beautiful earthen
smell when rain stops.
Flowers, flowers
blooming and blooming.
Ice cream sales
zooming and zooming;
Summer! Summer!
we wait all year
come on, hurry up
and get here.

M E Turner

GIVE ME

Give me the days,
The warmth on my face
As we walk through spring's open gates,
Let us shed the garb that we adorn,
As the roses dress their prickly thorn.

Give me the smell that summer brings,
As we splash in the sea, the pool, the rain,
As the butterflies float and the wasp stings,
Will this be the one that never ends?

Give me the sounds, the sights, the tastes,
As we live outdoors and play the games,
Of ball and bat, of sizzle and sip
And to the coast just one more trip.

Give me the heat as we remember
When we shivered last November,
So when we blister and when we thirst
I won't be long 'till October first.

Helene Pickering

SUMMER FETE AT THE PRIMARY SCHOOL

Enviably untyrannised by time,
The children stand in queues for painted faces,
To imitate beasts from overseas climes.

Two plucky boys climb up and straddle a pole
And, armed with pillows, beat each other off -
Down to a safety mat, both fighters roll.

Because the teachers moaned about chalk lost
From blackboards to redraw hopscotch grids, groundsmen
Marked yellow squares out, for a paltry cost.

Some dandelions have turned to clocks, and wait
For someone to get bored enough, and blow one.
They'll still be here tomorrow, round the gate!

Gillian Fisher

SPRING IN IRELAND

A golden freshness - spring is here
As daffodils wave and ring good cheer.
The long clear evenings brighten up
The emerald isle like a golden cup.

The snowy white lambs they skip and leap
The air is full of their gleeful bleat.
Through sun and shower - their carpet neat
A field of green - a green serene.

The hedgerows burst into bud and leaf
The birds they twitter in loft and tree.
The clouds are wafted far away,
Spring in Ireland is a heavenly day.

Elizabeth Jones

BROWNIE BLACKBERRIES

Blackberries, blackberries who will buy?
The black juicy ones fit for a pie
Picked by brownies at the break of day
Long before children come out to play.

Ho there witches the berries are cheap
Cook them today for they will not keep
Ho there pixies now is your chance
Make blackberry jellies for your next dance.

Hey little elves there are some left for you
Mix them with sugar and silvery dew
Blackberries, blackberries fine and sweet
Here I go selling them all down the street.

Marion Paton

THOUGHTS OF SUMMER

Tick tock - the clock's go on -
Summer time has just begun.
Blossom appearing on the trees,
Sounds of the busy honey bees.
Birds on branches, songs fill the air.
Children playing without a care.
Picnics taken in meadows green -
Nature here, all to be seen.

Cars towing caravans
Queues up ahead -
Motorway cones!
No stopping zones!
Laugher changes to moans.
Everyone sits with tired faces
All returning home.
Thinks, no more to roam.

But tomorrow dawns a brand new day -
Farmers out collecting hay.
Families all forget their moans,
Packing up to leave their homes.
Spending days upon beach -
Leaving troubles out of reach.

Margaret M France

SUMMER DAYS

They are nearly here, they are on the way.
Those lazy hazy summer days.
I love the warmth of the sun,
Walks in the park.
Nights that aren't dark.
Bathing costumes, swims in the sea.
Fish and chips and cream cakes for tea.
Ice cream and candy floss.
Is a must for days at the sea.
Children playing in the sand,
The band playing music in the bandstand
What lovely delights and the fairy lights.
Those magical, warm, happy days are on the way.
Oh, those lovely, hazy, lazy days of summer.

Ena Stanmore

ON THE BEACH

Red-faced mums and dogs with rabies
Razor pebbles, sunburnt babies
Bikini clad on summer beaches
Young girls perch on rain-washed bleachers.
Sandflies skeeter up your nose,
Damp grey mud between your toes
Noisy kids annoy their mums
Grit in swimsuits, up their bums
Oil skinned surfers do their stuff
Anglers call the fishes' bluff
Holiday makers changing diapers
Ice cream merchants play Pied Pipers.

Spiralled shells gleam in noon sun
Surrounding dogs and Englishmen
Crabs nip at toes out of reach
Dodging rubbish on the beach
Old crisp packets, torn tin foil
Empty tubs of sun tan oil
Broken masts from storm tossed ships
Purple packs from walnut whips
Seaweed chokes the weathered signs
Stating litter bugs risk fines
Swimmers having lots of fun
Trying not to swallow scum.

Deckchairs cushion wrinkled seats
Bathers pealing socks from feet
Try to change beneath a towel
Lotion laid on with a trowel
Cold chip butties fill with sand
Ice cream cones slip from wet hands
Swimming trunks leak folds of fat
Old men in their Panama hats.

Buckets filled up with sea water,
Father buried by his daughter
Little children with spades fumble
As their mighty towers crumble.

Mist horizon far away
Where the larger vessels stay
Yachtsmen hoisting yellowed sails
See sun worshippers as beached whales.
Big guys in their small shorts flex
Want the girls to see their pecs
Heat stroked maids in search of men
Sun, sea, sand and back for Ten
Frolic brainless in the dunes
Radios bang out jungle tunes
Women wish that they were thin
Darkness falls, the tide comes in.

Nick Smith

THE START OF SUMMER

Summer time starts after spring with a hop
A one hour jump forward upon the clock
Whether the sun shines or it does not
Clouds will determine all our lot
Temperatures will rise and the grass will grow
To give a green carpet instead of white snow
Flowers will bloom in colours, lovely and bright
In gardens and shows are a pleasing sight
Fruit and vegetables come to meet all our needs
There is always enough plus next years seeds
Weather forecasters predict and sometimes say
Sunny and bright for some of the day
Winds from the south will be gentle and light
But temperatures will drop with ground frost through the night
Then from time to time, it's cloudy with rain
An unsettled mixture, oh what a pain
Year after year on it goes
What next, only God knows.

Trevor Oates

GOODBYE TO WINTER

I lift my face towards the sun
And thank God spring has finally come.
No more chill winds to freeze my heart,
Or long, dark nights since we've been apart.

The warm gentle feel of sunshine on my skin
Caressing, soothing and now I can begin
To gently blow the past away with the breeze
A new season, a new start, a new sense of peace.

New found beauty in everything I see,
Mother Nature in all her glory calling out to me.
I close my eyes and softly breathe the sweet smell of her scent,
It fills my senses and my mind and now I feel that this was meant,
For no longer shall I grieve for a love affair gone wrong,
Spring arrives to bring new life,
The winter has now gone.

Irene McCready

SUMMER DAYS

Those sunny days are nature's way
To warm the earth, to ripen hay
To bring joy to children's faces
Sunday picnics, egg and spoon races
Flowers in their princely bloom
Bring sweet fragrance to any room
Long days sharing with life's best friend
Hoping summer will never end
Great planet shining oh! So bright
Follows us from morning on to night
We hope your power will never fail
As we swim, paddling, sail.

William B Dyer

A Glance Of Summer

The sweet smell of flowers
Freshly budding in the spring.
The true indication that summer will begin.
The sun begins to burn so strong
Bringing in the light
But when the day starts closing in
And nights begin to dawn
The sun it hides its shining face
And lets the darkness fall.

As we stroll along the sandy shore
And hear waves upon the sea
We look to see the shimmering glow
Which the moon provides for thee.
It gives us warmth
It gives us light and guides us on our way
And takes us on the trail to find the coming
Summer's day.

Lisa Doherty

INHERITANCE

Don't go out to play today
The sun is shining bright.
Don't go down to the sea today
The fish are slimy white.
Don't go out in the rain today
The rain will burn your skin.
This world is dying fast my son
And your father is to blame.
I have killed this earth, my son,
By slash, and burn and hack.
I have turned the green to brown
But you can bring it back.
You owe it to your children, son
To undo what I have done.
Let them inherit clean rain, my son
Let them inherit the sun.
This world is old and sick, my son
This earth is nearly done.
But you can clean the rivers son
And you can grow the trees
And then your son's will thank you son,
And their children will walk in
The rain, my son and swim in a clear clean sea.
They will sit on bright green
Grass and sniff the fresh clean air.
Son undo what I have done my
Son, undo what I have done.
You owe it to your children, son,
And to your children's sons.
I have never touched an elephant,
Or seen a squirrel run.
I have never seen an otter swim
In a clear, clean stream.
I have never seen an eagle soar
Or watched a badger romp.

I have never heard a lion roar
Or seen a flight of doves,
I've never seen the great white whale
Swim freely in the sea.
I have never walked in a great
Green forest and heard the
Blackbird sing.
I have never felt the pure clean
Rain upon my upturned face.
But I have seen the dark
Dead leaves in this filthy, dirty place.
I have seen the blood red sea
And feathers on a hat.
I have seen a bear skin rug and
Ivory by the ton.
But I have never touched an
Elephant or seen that squirrel run.

John Stenning

So Much Fun

Summer time is so much fun,
On the beach, trying not to catch the sun!

Mum's in the garden,
Planting lots of seeds,
My little brother's helping her,
Pulling out the weeds.

I can stay up longer,
The sun's still in the sky,
But eventually I fall asleep
Dreaming that I can fly.

I wake up in the morning,
The sun blinding my eyes,
The one bad thing about summer,
Is . . . I can't eat mince pies!

Ann Wilson (11)

DEDICATED TO MAX

Hi, Max, it's summer again
I miss you so much, lover and friend
Remember last summer with a smile
Although you was with us just a short while.
Remember the days we had in the sun
Played with the kids, had so much fun.
God took you on a dark winter's day
The hurt gets less, people say.
Think of the good times that we had
Forget the times that were sometimes bad.
Cos summer is a healing time
How I wish you was still mine
But let's be glad we had that time
And thank God it was summertime.
The smell of flowers and grass that's mown
The jobs you did around the home
I planted a rose bush just for you
Summer's bringing it out in bloom
Happy times in skies so blue
Summer loving special with you.

Lynn Gater

SUMMERTIME

Farewell to spring, May blossoms fade
And sun warmed earth erupts.
Abundant greenery spreads far and wide.
Caressed with gentle summer rain, a myriad
Range of coloured blooms face upwards to the sky above
Where deep or pastel shades of blue are but a
Stage for snow white clouds to dance aloft.
Below, in copse and woodland moist and cool,
Deer gently graze.
The lazy dragon flies float on the sultry breeze,
Amid the sound of honey bees.
Idyllic, warm and peaceful days,
Not timeless.
Enjoy! Enjoy! Before the harvest
Moon appears.

John Robinson

BRITISH SUMMERTIME

'Remember the clocks,' shout the children
'Shall we do them tonight before bed?'
'No leave them till morning,' I grumbled
'Leave it till later,' I said
'Can we do them right now' ask the children
No just get your cornflakes instead''
'I'll see to them all in a minute
We've only just got out of bed.'
'I'll do the cuckoo' shouts Billy
'I'll do the kitchen' yells Ben
'Fix the alarm' bellows Susie
'It's scaring me out of my head'
'There's the one in the car, that one's dodgy
There's the video, that one is bad
And the carriage clock Aunty Sue gave us
Is looking left over and sad.'
'There's the cooker, let Mum do the cooker
And the microwave, I can do that'
'Ben better do the computer
Or his Email will simply go flat.'
'By the time that we've finished,' I grumble
'The summer will pass us all by
We'll be changing them back in the autumn
What's the point I never know why?'

Judy Smith

AT THE BEACH IN SUMMER

The sun comes out
to the beach we run.
Everyone is out
now summer has begun.

Children carrying buckets
and their spades.
Transistor radios
Being played.

Sat on deck chairs
with the windbreaker up.
Drinking pop from
a sandy cup.

Making sandcastles, cars,
and a boat.
Carrying back water
to make the castle's moat.

Ice creams that dribble down
seagulls that hover around.
Seashells of every kind
appear in the bright sunshine.

Lying on a towel
in the warm sun.
Hearing donkeys jingle
as they run.

Writing messages
in the sand.
Walking bare foot
hand in hand.
Summertime is grand.

Lisa Kelly

An Evocation Of Summer

Now what does summer mean to me?
Does it speak of sand and open sea?
Do nesting birds and basking frogs
And churning tadpoles round floating logs,
Evoke a sense of summer come
Or does it just mean winter's done?

For me a sign that summer's come
Is lying flat and viewing sun,
Through half closed eyes and tracery
Of branches of some ancient tree;
And listening to the birds that sing
From roosts nearby, or on the wing.

And when on summer mornings still,
Walking through dew, my sandals fill;
To sense the freshness all around,
Of summer sent and nature bound.

Jean Rosemary Regan

FIREFLIES

Thick, wet heat chokes the air;
Twentieth century swamp dwellers
Are living slowly through a sauna summer,
Out in velvety Virginia nights
That touch your face, demanding reaction,
In communion with the acrid chocolate earth.
Cicadas fill the air with their peculiar melody,
Baritone bullfrogs declare their virility,
The natural history of love is here
We give our embrace to this creation orgy.

As the stage is set the dancers come,
A perfect festival of lights they move
Through cracks in the blanket darkness,
Hidden children delight in this magical weave.
Tiny frames burn with loving radiation,
They are alight with that which burns in me,
Drinking in each detail of the other, we
Search for elusive sparks in each other's eyes,
Strange how our lovefire shows itself in tears
Standing in ovation to the fireflies.

Jemma Richards

WELL - IT'S SUMMER, ISN'T IT?

Predictable, it's simply not,
Sometimes cold, sometimes hot.
But winter now, sees life at ease,
Nothing expected, no one displeased.
Just cold, wet, windy and mean,
No shocks, now that's a predictable scene.

How people long for the summertime
Dreams of beaches and days sublime,
But are we happy? Not a chance,
That season leads us a merry dance.
Will it? Won't it? Clouds and sun
Play hide and seek till the day is done.

Till we're weary of watching and having to wait
For the next fine day when we hold the fete.
And it generally rains and the lawn's a lake
And it generally rains on our two weeks break.
And we sit at our desks while the sun beats down
And everyone else is getting brown.

Long limbed lovelies in briefest shorts,
For the less than lovely, spare a thought,
For the chubby, the sweaty, the chefs and cooks,
The weather plays havoc with clothes and looks,
But smile! It's summer! Don't wear a frown,
It's just not allowed, so wave, don't drown!

Audrey Loftin

HEAT WAVE

The temperature is soaring
Dad's flaked out and snoring
Mum's in her bikini getting brown.

The pollen makes me sneeze
I wish there was a breeze
Or some rainfall to cool me down.

The sky's electric blue
Not a single cloud in view
To protect us from the sun's scorching rays.

I'm sticky and I'm wet
Even thinking makes me sweat
So I'll find a shady tree and simply laze.

S Brewer

WISH YOU WERE HERE

Summer postcards from foreign climes
Bring all the magic of happy times,
By friends who travel on a holiday
'Wish you were here' - is what they say.

'Wish you were here' - the weather's fine
The food is good, dinner at nine.
The boat trips out along the shore
The days will pass, 'twill soon be o'er.

These little snippets keep us in touch
An added greeting means so much.
'Looking forward to seeing you soon'
The latest card is postmarked the moon.

Mary Josephine Devlin

SPRING

As my eyes gaze up, I can clearly see,
What joys and wonders spring has given to me,
The tiny, fluffy bunnies, now seen all around,
Their little tails bobbing, not making a sound,
The new budded blossoms, on the gentle old tree,
Now newly clothed, it means so much to me,
The spring showers forgotten on the newly grown grass,
A season ago, a barren ground, it's forgotten, past,
After the death of winter, comes the whole earth's rebirth,
A new sense of beginning now circles the earth,
Time now for the happiness that the spring has sprung,
Now that Old Man Winter has sung his song.

Sarah Louise Woodard

SUMMER

Summer is a-coming, put your glad rags on,
Say goodbye to winter, dark clouds have gone.
Holidays at the seaside, digging in the sand,
Walking along the prom, holding one another's hand.

The sun shining brightly, in a cloudless sky,
Thinking of our loved ones, how they went and why,
Abroad, for a hot climate, so they could get a tan,
We're going to Blackpool, to see a very funny man.

We'll look forward to the sunshine, many hours we hope,
Our friends have gone to Italy, hoping to see the Pope.
We're saving on expenses and having a break at home,
Out in the summer sunshine, through the fields we'll roam.

I'll look forward to the summer, the cold I couldn't stand,
With snow and Jack Frost around, nipping at my hand.
Now the season has changed, hopefully for the best,
Hot weather, lots of sunshine and a jolly good rest.

Of course, we shall have rain, to keep the dust down,
You'll see it in the country but seldom in the town.
Warm rain to feed the plants, because they like a drink
And we can admire the flowers, carnations, red and pink.

Summer and dry weather, children playing on the swings,
Dad, messing in the garden, fiddling with different things.
The nights staying lighter, now we've put the hour on,
We'll make the most of days, before the summer's gone.

So it's sunshine, blue skies, no dull clouds anymore,
We're going to have a heatwave, this year, that's for sure.
You can bet some will be moaning, when it gets too hot
But we've got to have what comes, the sun, the rain, the lot.

So this is the end of my summer poem, I hope it will do,
I like writing poetry and I hope you'll read my rhyme too.

Will Jebb

MY KIND OF SUMMER

Ice-cream treats
and tasty sweets
My kind of summer

Bird songs you can hear
celebrations far to near

Some say they're hotter
so they hear
I can't wait until next year!

Zoe House (11)

AS SUMMER APPROACHES

As summer approaches,
A sense of enthusiasm fills the air,
As winter draws its last breath,
The cold, wet days are left to thaw by summer's feverish heat,
Flowers in full bloom drift through the long hours,
Gazing at the fire that sets the sky ablaze,
And then the sun sets,
Mixing colours as it sinks into a far-off hill,
Leaving a cool crisp night . . .
                                        Summer has arrived.

Daniel Lynch (14)

SUBMISSIONS INVITED
SOMETHING FOR EVERYONE

POETRY NOW 2000 - Any subject,
any style, any time.

WOMENSWORDS 2000 - Strictly women,
have your say the female way!

STRONGWORDS 2000 - Warning!
Age restriction, must be between 16-24,
opinionated and have strong views.
(Not for the faint-hearted)

All poems no longer than 30 lines.
Always welcome! No fee!
Cash Prizes to be won!

Mark your envelope (eg *Poetry Now) 2000*
Send to:
Forward Press Ltd
Remus House, Coltsfoot Drive,
Woodston,
Peterborough, PE2 9JX

OVER £10,000 POETRY PRIZES
TO BE WON!

Judging will take place in October 2000